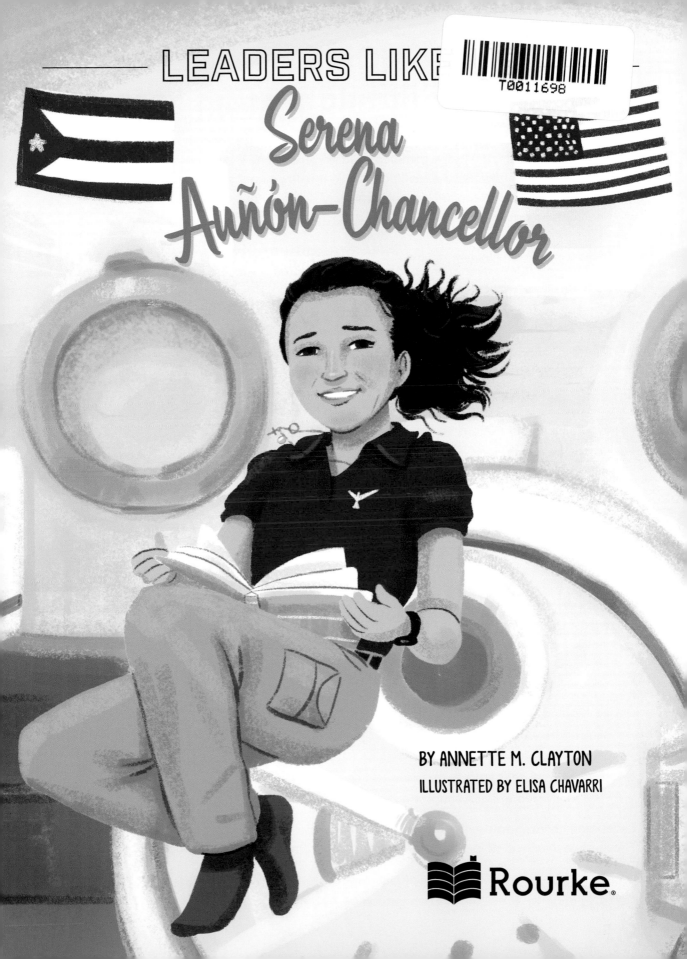

LEADERS LIKE US

Serena Auñón-Chancellor

BY ANNETTE M. CLAYTON

ILLUSTRATED BY ELISA CHAVARRI

Rourke.

Before Reading: *Building Background Knowledge and Vocabulary*

Building background knowledge can help children process new information and build upon what they already know. Before reading a book, it is important to tap into what children already know about the topic. This will help them develop their vocabulary and increase their reading comprehension.

Questions and Activities to Build Background Knowledge:

1. Look at the front cover of the book and read the title. What do you think this book will be about?
2. What do you already know about this topic?
3. Take a book walk and skim the pages. Look at the table of contents, photographs, captions, and bold words. Did these text features give you any information or predictions about what you will read in this book?

Vocabulary: *Vocabulary Is Key to Reading Comprehension*

Use the following directions to prompt a conversation about each word.

- Read the vocabulary words.
- What comes to mind when you see each word?
- What do you think each word means?

> ### Vocabulary Words:
> - aerospace
> - astronaut
> - candidate
> - engineer
> - experiments
> - immigrated
> - launch
> - samples

During Reading: *Reading for Meaning and Understanding*

To achieve deep comprehension of a book, children are encouraged to use close reading strategies. During reading, it is important to have children stop and make connections. These connections result in deeper analysis and understanding of a book.

 ## Close Reading a Text

During reading, have children stop and talk about the following:

- Any confusing parts
- Any unknown words
- Text to text, text to self, text to world connections
- The main idea in each chapter or heading

Encourage children to use context clues to determine the meaning of any unknown words. These strategies will help children learn to analyze the text more thoroughly as they read.

When you are finished reading this book, turn to the next-to-last page for **Text-Dependent Questions** and an **Extension Activity**.

TABLE OF CONTENTS

DREAMS OF THE STARS

Have you ever had more than one dream? How could you make them both come true?

Serena wanted to work for NASA (National Aeronautics and Space Administration). She also wanted to become a doctor. But could she do both? Yes! Meet Serena Auñón-Chancellor, a NASA **astronaut** and a doctor. Serena is a leader in **aerospace** medicine.

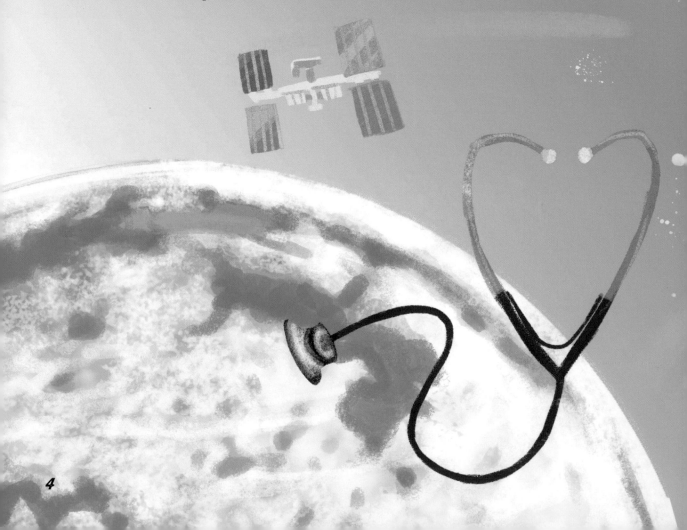

Serena's heart thumped. She grabbed the spacecraft's handle and ducked inside. Soon, she would be blasting off into space! Ever since she was little, Serena dreamed about this moment.

She worked hard and studied even harder.

Today, her dream was coming true. Serena and her crew would **launch** into space. Then, they would connect with the International Space Station (ISS).

The road to becoming an astronaut was filled with twists and turns. But for Serena, it was worth it.

BORN TO FLY

Serena was born on April 9, 1976, in Indiana. Her father **immigrated** from Cuba to the United States. As a child, Serena watched a rocket soar into space. It filled her with wonder. Her father asked if she wanted to work for NASA one day. Serena told him she did.

NASA has many different types of jobs. Serena's father was an electrical **engineer**. So, he suggested she study engineering.

After high school, Serena remembered her father's advice. She studied electrical engineering in college. Her astronaut dreams were getting closer! But then, something surprising happened.

Serena had many friends who studied medicine. They told Serena she would make an excellent doctor. Serena thought about it . . . they were right! Serena realized she loved space and medicine.

After college, she set off to get another degree. This time to become a doctor.

HIDDEN TALENTS

To earn money in college, Serena taught kung fu to kids ages 5-15 about three times a week.

In 2006, Serena joined the Johnson Space Center as a doctor. She spent nine months in Russia caring for astronauts.

Serena enjoyed being a doctor. But still, her heart belonged to the stars.

She decided to apply for NASA's astronaut program. This was her chance to go into space! But there was one moon-sized problem—over 3,000 people applied.

Shooting stars bounced in her belly. Did she have a shot? Finally, Serena got the news . . . she was accepted!

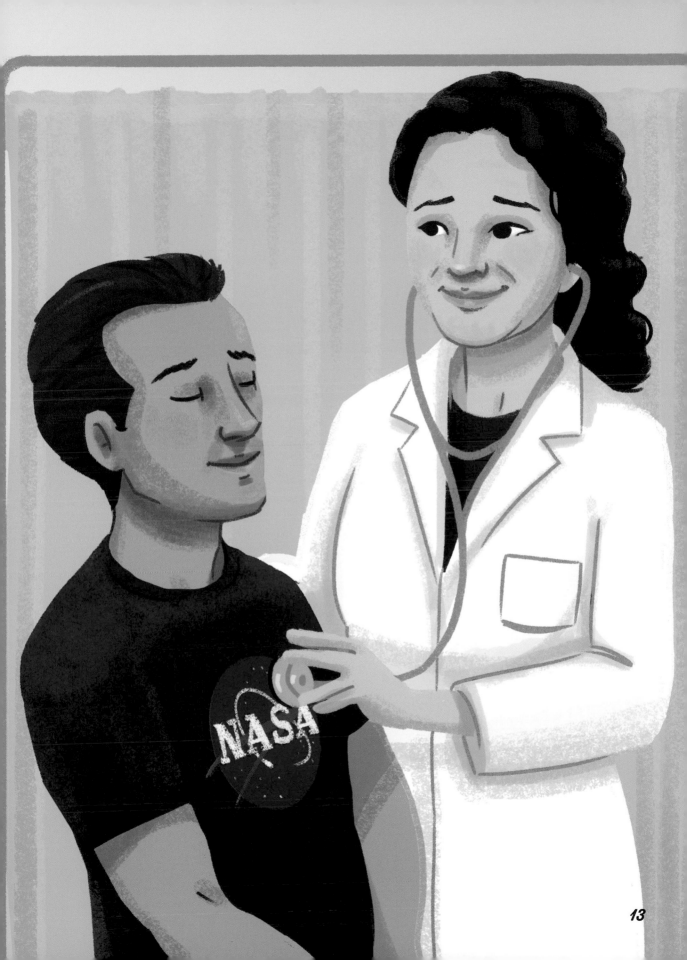

ROCKETING TO SUCCESS

Serena became an astronaut **candidate**, which is an astronaut in training. There was still so much to learn! For two years Serena trained. She learned everything—

from space station systems...
...to robotics and space walks...
...to wilderness survival skills.

Serena was prepared.

TOUGH TRAINING

NASA sends astronauts to train in extreme environments. Serena spent several weeks in an undersea vehicle. She was also stationed in Antarctica for two months. Surviving in harsh conditions helps astronauts mentally prepare for emergencies in space.

Serena finished training and took exams. She passed with flying colors. Serena was now an astronaut! But she wasn't going to space just yet. She had to wait for her space assignment.

In 2017, Serena got a phone call from NASA. She held her breath. It was the news she had been waiting for. Finally, she was going to space!

LAUNCHING A LEADER

Serena trained to fly on the Soyuz spacecraft. It would take Serena and the crew to the ISS.

On June 6, 2018, Serena heard the countdown begin— 3, 2, 1, blast off! The rocket shot into space. Serena looked at the beautiful Earth below.

Serena performed many **experiments** in space. She researched changes to the human body. She also studied cancer treatments.

SPACE SCIENCE

Serena conducted experiments for scientists on Earth. Sometimes, she was the experiment. She collected **samples** of her blood, saliva, urine, and poop to study. It wasn't easy. In space, these things float!

Serena was in outer space for 197 days. She was the second Latina to launch to the stars.

Now that she's back on Earth, Serena is still busy. She is a teacher and gives speeches around the world. In her free time, she volunteers at a free clinic in Texas.

Sometimes though, she just sits back . . .

and watches the stars.

" People think science we do on the space station only relates to space exploration. They don't realize how much it matters to medical care of everyday living here on Earth. — Serena Auñón-Chancellor "

TIME LINE

1976   Serena is born April 9th in Indianapolis, Indiana.

1993   Serena graduates from Poudre High School,
Fort Collins, Colorado.

1997   Serena receives a Bachelor of Science in Electrical
Engineering from The George Washington University.

2001   Serena graduates as a Doctor of Medicine from
The University of Texas Health Science Center at Houston.

2006   Serena joins the Johnson Space Center in August as a
Flight Surgeon.

2009   Serena is selected by NASA as an astronaut candidate.

2009   Serena receives the United States Air Force Flight Surgeons
Julian Ward Award.

2010   Serena spends two months in Antarctica searching for
meteorites as part of the ANSMET expedition.

2012   Serena operates the Deep Worker submersible as part of
the NEEMO 16 mission.

2017   Serena is inducted into the Space Camp Hall of Fame.

2018   Serena launches into space!

2019   Serena begins teaching at Louisiana State University.

GLOSSARY

aerospace (AIR-oh-spase): having to do with the science and technology of space travel

astronaut (AS-truh-nawt): someone who travels in a spacecraft

candidate (KAN-di-date): someone who applies for a job or runs in an election

engineer (en-juh-NEER): someone who has been trained to design and build machines or large structures

experiments (ik-SPER-uh-ments): tests to try out a theory or to see the effect of something

immigrated (im-i-GRAY-ted): to have come to another country to live permanently

launch (lawnch): to send a rocket or missile into space

samples (SAM-puhls): small parts of something that show what the whole is like

INDEX

TEXT-DEPENDENT QUESTIONS

1. What were some of the things Serena studied in astronaut training?

2. Name one job Serena had after being an astronaut.

3. Why was Serena nervous when she applied for NASA's astronaut program?

4. What did Serena study while in space?

EXTENSION ACTIVITY

Serena conducted scientific experiments while in space. Design an experiment you would like to do while floating around a spaceship. Here are some examples: Would an ice cube melt faster in space or on Earth? Would your singing voice sound different in zero-gravity or the same?

ABOUT THE AUTHOR

Annette M. Clayton is an author living in Maryland with her twin daughters, husband, and one fluffy cat. She has Puerto Rican roots and hopes to share stories that will inspire children's imaginations, spark creativity, and foster inclusivity. One of her favorite activities is hiking on the Appalachian Trail. When it's too cold for that, you can find her inside, drinking lattes and reading a good book.

ABOUT THE ILLUSTRATOR

Elisa Chavarri is an award-winning illustrator who strives to create work that inspires happiness, promotes inclusiveness and curiosity, and helps people of all different backgrounds feel special. She has illustrated numerous books for children including the Pura Belpré Honor book *Sharuko: El Arqueólogo Peruano/Peruvian Archaeologist Julio C. Tello.* Elisa hails from Lima, Peru, and resides in Alpena, Michigan, with her husband and two young children.

www.rourkebooks.com

PHOTO CREDITS: page 20: 2020 Images / Alamy Stock Photo

Quote source: Argueta, Erica. "Space medicine isn't just for astronauts. It's for all of us." *CNET*, Sept. 2019, https://www.cnet.com/science/features/space-medicine-isnt-just-for-astronauts-its-for-all-of-us/#ftag=COS-05-10aaa0j.

Edited by: Hailey Scragg
Illustrations by: Elisa Chavarri
Cover and interior layout by: J.J. Giddings

Library of Congress PCN Data

Serena Auñón-Chancellor / Annette M. Clayton
(Leaders Like Us)
ISBN 978-1-73165-770-1 (hard cover) (alk. paper)
ISBN 978-1-73165-773-2 (soft cover)
ISBN 978-1-73165-775-6 (e-book)
ISBN 978-1-73165-777-0 (e-pub)
Library of Congress Control Number: 2023942365

Rourke Educational Media
Printed in the United States of America
01-0152411937